The Palace of Minos at Knossos

digging
for the past

BRIAN FAGAN
General Editor

The Palace of Minos at Knossos

Chris Scarre and Rebecca Stefoff

OXFORD

UNIVERSITY PRESS

To Zachary, my partner in exploring Crete

OXFORD
UNIVERSITY PRESS

Oxford   New York
Auckland   Bangkok   Buenos Aires   Cape Town   Chennai
Dar es Salaam   Delhi   Hong Kong   Istanbul   Karachi   Kolkata
Kuala Lumpur   Madrid   Melbourne   Mexico City   Mumbai   Nairobi
São Paulo   Shanghai   Singapore   Taipei   Tokyo   Toronto

Published by Oxford University Press, Inc.
198 Madison Avenue, New York, New York 10016
www.oup-usa.org

Oxford is a registered trademark of Oxford University Press

Design: Kingsley Parker
Layout: Lenny Levitsky

Library of Congress Cataloging-in-Publication Data

Scarre, Christopher.
  The Palace of Minos at Knossos / Chris Scarre and Rebecca Stefoff.
     p. cm. — (Digging for the past)
Summary: Discusses the ancient Minoan civilization of Knossos, Crete, as
manifested by the excavations of that city by the archaeologist Sir
Arthur Evans.
Includes bibliographical references and index.
  ISBN 0-19-514272-1 (alk. paper) — ISBN 0-19-514272-1 (alk. paper)
  1. Palace of Knossos (Knossos)—Juvenile literature. 2. Knossos
(Extinct city)—Juvenile literature. 3. Excavations
(Archaeology)—Greece—Knossos (Extinct city)—Juvenile literature. 4.
Evans, Arthur, Sir, 1851-1941—Juvenile literature. 5. Crete
(Greece)—Antiquities—Juvenile literature. [1. Palace of Knossos
(Knossos) 2. Knossos (Extinct city) 3. Crete (Greece)—Antiquities. 4.
Excavations (Archaeology)—Greece. 5. Evans, Arthur, Sir, 1851-1941.]
I. Stefoff, Rebecca, 1951- II. Title. III. Series.
  DF221.C8 S238 2003
  728.8'2'093918—dc21

                                          2003003712

9 8 7 6 5 4 3 2 1
Printed in Hong Kong on acid-free paper

Picture Credits: Giraudon/Art Resource, NY: 28, 36; Erich Lessing/Art Resource, NY: 8, 12,
25, 26, 29, 33; Nimatallah/Art Resource, NY: 26; Ashmolean Museum, Oxford: cover inset,
2–3, 10, 15, 17, 18, 19, 20, 23, 24, 32, 37; Saul S. Weinburg Collection, Boston University
Department of Archaeology: cover, 9; British School at Athens: 30; Corbis: 22; © C/Z HAR-
RIS: 1, 3 (inset), 14, 27, 40 (bottom), 42; Laserwords Graphics: 6, 34 (adopted from illus-
tration by François Brosse in Alexandria Farnoux's Knossos: Search for the Legendary Palace of King
Minos), 39; Courtesy of Chris Scarre: 42 (top); Amy C. Smith: 31; © Time Pix: 11

Contents

Where and When   6

CHAPTER 1
An Unexplored World   8

CHAPTER 2
Discovering a Lost Palace   16

CHAPTER 3
In Search of the Minoans   25

CHAPTER 4
Knossos Today   31

Interview with Chris Scarre   40

Glossary   43

Further Reading   44

Related Sites   45

Index   47

Where and When

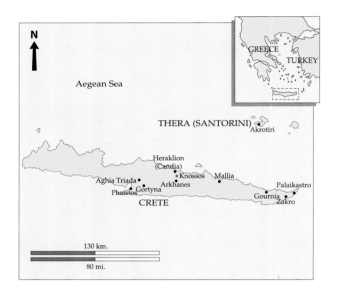

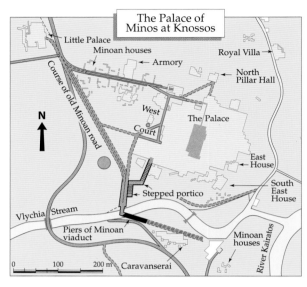

The Palace of
Minos at Knossos

Archaeological History

1886 ▶
Archaeologist Heinrich Schliemann visits Crete and tries to gain control of Knossos site

◀ **1897**
Minos Kalokairinos recovers large jars and other artifacts from Kephala hill, legendary site of Knossos

1900–1905 ▶
Arthur Evans begins excavating Knossos on March 23, 1900; most of the palace structure is excavated

◀ **1906**
Evans builds Villa Ariadne as his residence at Knossos

1920s ▶
Evans oversees reconstruction of many parts of the palace with reinforced concrete

◀ **1921–35**
Evans publishes *The Palace of Minos at Knossos* in four volumes

1941 ▶
Evans dies in England

◀ **1952**
Michael Ventris and John Chadwick decipher Linear B, an early version of Greek language used at Knossos and other Minoan sites

1979 ▶
British and Greek archaeologists uncover evidence of human sacrifice in Minoan Crete

◀ **1990s**
New conservation techniques are introduced to preserve both Minoan ruins and Evans's restorations

Ancient History

7000 B.C.E.	◀ First known habitation at Knossos
3000–2000 B.C.E.	◀ Use of stone as building material increases; town in existence
2000–1800s B.C.E.	◀ Old or First Palace is built; Knossos emerges as center of Minoan civilization
1700 B.C.E.	◀ Old Palace period ends in destructive fire; the palace of Knossos (essentially the same structure visible today) is rebuilt on grander scale
1600–1500 B.C.E.	◀ High point of Minoan culture and influence; architecture and decorative style of Knossos reflected throughout Crete and as far away as Egypt; Throne Room and major frescoes designed
1480 B.C.E.	◀ Earthquake rocks and destroys Cretan palaces; only Knossos survives; former palace chambers become storage compartments or crafts workshops
1450–1380 B.C.E.	◀ Mycenaeans from mainland Greece take over administration of Knossos
1370 B.C.E.	◀ Major fire at Knossos
1250 B.C.E.	◀ Central administration of palace ends; parts of Knossos become uninhabited

1

An Unexplored World

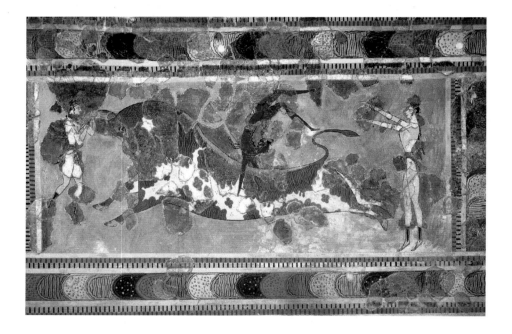

One of the best-known and most mysterious wall paintings from Knossos shows the acrobatic and extremely dangerous art of bull-leaping. Archaeologists do not know whether such feats really took place in the ancient palace.

The sprawling palace of Knossos gleamed white in the spring sunshine. The smooth, painted columns that supported its flat roofs glowed a rich red. Excited men and women were crowded around the Great Court, intent on the thrilling spectacle before them.

The ground trembled as a bull thundered past. Then several young men and women appeared. Their long black hair was gathered into top knots, with ringlets hanging down their backs. Slender and lithe, these athletes looked small next to the massive animal. The crowd gasped with awe and dread as a young man ran directly toward the charging bull and leaped into the air. He turned a somersault above the great beast, flipping his heels over his head and balancing for an instant with his hands on the bull's back before dropping lightly to his feet behind it.

Scenes of bulls and acrobatic athletes were painted on the walls of Knossos. Some modern researchers believe that bull-leaping occurred just as it is shown in the paintings. Others argue that the paintings represent scenes from mythology, not real events. The palace and the people who lived in it, however, were very real.

They were the Minoans, a centuries-old civilization on the island of Crete. The Minoans were the supreme seafarers of the Mediterranean in 1550 B.C.E., with a far-ranging fleet of merchant ships. They would never have believed that their civilization would soon crumble or that they would be all but forgotten. Almost 3,400 years would pass before someone uncovered their long-buried

Set amid hills near Crete's northern coast, Knossos has had two identities for more than a century. It is a site of ongoing archaeo-logical discovery and one of the most popular tourist destinations in the Mediterranean world.

Arthur Evans seemed an unlikely adventurer, but he was inquisitive, energetic, and fond of travel off the beaten track. In this fanciful 1907 porrtrait by Sir W. B. Richmond, Evans is surrounded by Minoan art that includes decorated pottery and a brightly colored fresco behind him. Today, the Minoans are well-known for their bright, energetically flowing painted walls.

palace and revealed the vanished glories of their way of life.

The excavator of the palace at Knossos was an Englishman named Arthur John Evans. Born into a wealthy family, Evans grew up with archaeology. His father had a strong interest in ancient objects and young Evans sometimes accompanied his father to nearby sites to dig for them.

Arthur Evans studied history at Oxford University, with a special emphasis on the history of languages. He grew interested in obscure and little-known periods of ancient history. Evans wondered who the forerunners of the Greeks had been and what had happened in the Mediterranean world before the flowering of classical Greece.

Evans worked as a journalist in the Balkans, the mountainous area north of Greece. There he met and married Margaret Freeman, the daughter of an English historian.

The Evanses returned to England, where Arthur Evans became keeper of the Ashmolean Museum at Oxford University. Evans added artifacts that emphasize the social, ethnic, and archaeological aspects of the ancient world to the Ashmolean Museum's classical Greek and Roman collections, gathering some antiquities for new exhibits on long Mediterranean journeys.

Just before Evans began working at the Ashmolean, he and his wife toured Greece, where they visited the distinguished archaeologist Heinrich Schliemann. During the 1870s Schliemann had made two extraordinary discoveries, excavating the city of Troy in Asia Minor

(now Turkey) and the fortress-palace of Mycenae in southern Greece. Schliemann's method of archaeology was to look for places mentioned in ancient writings that others had long considered purely mythological. His findings unveiled a rich and sophisticated culture that flourished in Greece centuries before the beginning of recorded classical history. New vistas seemed to open into the distant past, and archaeologists looked around the Mediterranean for sites that might yield similar discoveries.

Fascinating references to Crete, a large island south of Greece, in ancient texts drew the attention of many. Some are clearly

Heinrich Schliemann shared his discoveries with the world through a flood of articles and books with illustrations. This drawing of graves at Mycenae shows the Schliemanns (in the center) examining the site. His successes inspired Evans to look for his own great find.

mythological—for example, the island was said to have been the haunt of monsters and the birthplace of Zeus, father and leader of the Greek gods. The best known legend told of a king named Minos, maker of laws and possessor of a strong army, who kept in a labyrinth, or maze, beneath his palace a monster called the Minotaur that was half man, half bull. According to the legend, the city of Athens on the Greek mainland had to send young men and women as sacrifices to the Minotaur until the mythic hero Theseus slew the monster.

A few references, however, hinted that Crete had played a role in Mediterranean history during the Bronze Age, before the rise of classical Greece. The Greek poet Homer wrote in *The Odyssey*,

Myths from the ancient Aegean world became part of the shared culture of Europeans. This mosaic, or picture made of small stones, comes from a Roman building of the first century C.E. in what is now Austria. At the center of the maze, Theseus slays the Minotaur.

"There is a land called Crete in the middle of the wine-blue water, a handsome country and fertile, seagirt, and there are many peoples in it, innumerable; there are ninety cities." *The Iliad*, the companion epic to *The Odyssey* and the poem that convinced Schliemann to dig for Troy, mentions a dance floor at Knossos, the palace of the kings of Crete.

Although Crete had passed consecutively into the hands of the Romans, the Christian empire of Byzantium, the Italian city-state of Venice, and finally the Muslim empire of the Ottomans, who ruled Turkey and much of the Middle East, the legend of the island's mighty king and his palace had never completely disappeared. Tradition said that Knossos had stood on Kephala, a hill near the northern coast of the island, not far from the port city the Venetians and the Ottomans called Candia (today it is Heraklion).

Visitors to Kephala often found coins bearing the word *Knosion*, a version of "Knossos," but they saw no monuments like the marble pillars and temples of classical Greece and Rome. A French scholar visited the site in 1857 and wrote,

> Knossos, the oldest city of ancient Crete, the one that ruled without rival, supreme overall the other, has left no ruins. On the southeastern heights above the small plain where Candia stands is one miserable village whose name, Makrytichos, or the Long Wall, informs the antiquarian that there were once great constructions here; but at most he can detect only the vague, formless debris of mounds of bricks.

In 1879 a Greek businessman and diplomat named Minos Kalokairinos excavated some *pithoi*, large jars used to store goods such as oil or grain, and sent samples to European museums to arouse interest in the site. The local government stopped Kalokairinos's excavation, fearing that any valuable relics he found

Dozens of large pithoi, or ceramic storage jars, have been found in the ruins of Knossos. Some still stand or lie where they were placed thousands of years ago when the palace was in use.

would be carried off by the hated Turkish overlords of the island. Although mainland Greece had won independence from the Turks in 1832, Crete remained under Turkish rule.

Schliemann visited Kephala twice in the 1880s and dreamed of ending his archaeological career by finding "the prehistoric palace of the kings of Knossos in Crete." Disputes with the Turkish authorities and the owners of the Kephala land prevented him from doing so. During the 1890s French, German, and Italian archaeologists competed for the right to excavate the site. At the same time, Arthur Evans was trying to buy it.

Evans's interest in Crete had grown over the years. In 1883 he had examined carved rings and small stones, called sealstones, that Schliemann had found at Mycenae. Pressed into wax or clay, they left designs that sealed an item such as letters or envelopes. Evans thought that some of the symbols on the sealstones reflected a style and culture other than Greek. Later he collected more seals and learned that many of them came from Crete, where they were so common that women wore them on necklaces. He began to suspect that the markings on the seals might be related to an early, unknown form of writing that had spanned the ancient Mediterranean world from Egypt to Mycenae.

In 1894 Evans visited Crete for the first time. On his first day he acquired 23 carved stones from a market in Heraklion. He also

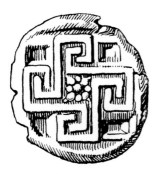

Evans sketched thousands of artifacts unearthed at Knossos, including these coins from a settlement at the site, centuries after the palace period. Two sketches (left, center) show images of mazes, or labyrinths, while one (right) features a Minotaur.

visited Kephala hill, the fabled site of Knossos, and saw broken pottery and many other signs of ancient occupation. Evans's wife had died the previous year, and his life in England had nothing to hold him. He decided to excavate Knossos.

During his attempt to purchase the site, an uprising against the Turks broke out across Crete in 1897 and brought the end of Turkish rule. Italy, Great Britain, France, and Russia became the temporary administrators of the island. It was later added to the Greek nation in 1913. By 1899, however, the excitement of the revolt had died down and Evans secured his claim to Kephala.

With the help of a skilled and experienced staff that included Scottish archaeologist Duncan Mackenzie, Evans began excavating on March 23, 1900. He had met Kalokairinos and discussed the site with him and he began his own work where Kalokairinos had excavated more than 20 years earlier. Evans did not have to wait long for results—the first day's work turned up artifacts and the buried remains of buildings. Almost from the first shovel-stroke Evans realized that Knossos was "an extraordinary phenomenon, nothing Greek, nothing Roman." He was stepping back in time to enter, as he later wrote, "a wholly unexplored world."

2

Discovering a Lost Palace

A newspaper announcement in 1899 invited the British public to contribute to the Cretan Exploration Fund. Evans was one of two directors of the Fund. The other was David Hogarth, head of the British School at Athens (BSA), an organization that promotes British study and archaeology in Greece. Evans hoped that the Fund would raise enough money to pay for the excavation and the cost of buying Kephala. To his dismay, it raised far less than he had anticipated.

In later years, the discoveries at Knossos would attract contributions to the Cretan Exploration Fund. But at first Evans bore the expenses himself, helped by frequent donations from his father. In some ways this pleased Evans, who wrote to his father in late 1900, "I am quite resolved not to have this thing entirely 'pooled' for several reasons, but largely because I must have sole control of what I am personally undertaking." Because Evans owned the land and paid the bills, he had total control over the work at Knossos. Evans regarded the ruins as his to uncover, interpret, and protect as he chose. Athough a new Cretan antiquities law required him to turn over most artifacts to the local government, he was allowed to keep minor finds.

On March 3, 1900, Evans and Mackenzie began their excavation by cutting into the top of the highest point on the center of Kephala where Kalokairinos had found *pithoi* in the ruins of what

The Cretan Exploration Fund.

Patron:
H.R.H. PRINCE GEORGE OF GREECE,
High Commissioner of the Powers in Crete.

Directors:

ARTHUR J. EVANS, M.A., F.S.A.,
Ashmole's Keeper, and Hon. Fellow of Brasenose College, Oxford.

DAVID G. HOGARTH, M.A., F.S.A., F.R.G.S.,
Fellow of Magdalen College, Oxford, and late Director of the British School at Athens.

R. CARR BOSANQUET, M.A., F.S.A.,
Director of the British School at Athens.

Hon. Treasurer:

GEORGE A. MACMILLAN,
Hon. Secretary of the Society for Promoting Hellenic Studies.

Hon. Secretary:

JOHN L. MYRES, M.A., F.S.A., F.R.G.S.,
Student of Christ Church, Oxford.

The Throne Room in the Palace at Knossos in course of Excavation.

The following Appeal, including a Statement of last Season's work, has been issued on behalf of the Fund:—

THE preoccupation of the public mind caused by the war in South Africa made it impossible last year to press the claims of Cretan exploration. Sympathy, indeed, was not wanting. A representative Committee was formed, and we were able to initiate a Fund, to which the patronage of the High Commissioner of the Powers in Crete, Prince George of Greece, was accorded. Thanks to the good offices of His Royal Highness, a number of important sites were set apart for British excavation. But of the £5,000

In 1900 the Cretan Exploration Fund published an appeal for contributions toward the work at Knossos. The photograph shows workers excavating the chamber that Evans dubbed the Throne Room.

A figure on a cross, a statue of the ancient goddess of love, or simply part of a female form? When workers dug up this small clay figurine (sketched by Evans), people at the site interpreted it in various ways—an example of how hard it can be to know the true uses and meanings of many ancient objects.

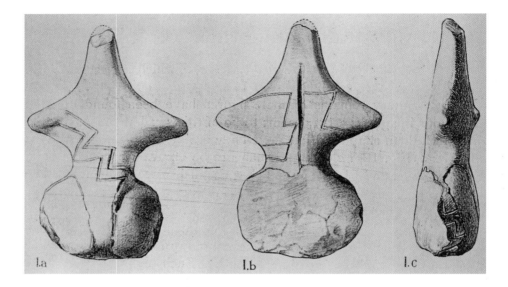

1.a   1.b   1.c

appeared to be a storeroom. Evans wanted to locate the floor and walls of the buried building. Workers were men from local villages, hired to wield pickaxes and shovels, sift baskets of earth for artifacts, and then dump the sifted earth on the hillsides.

In spite of Kalokairinos's finds and his own hopes, Evans had no guarantee that he would discover anything important at Knossos. But artifacts were plentiful. On the second day the diggers unearthed a small terracotta figurine. The varying responses to this find indicated that people's knowledge and expectations shaped their ideas about the discoveries at the site. The workers, both Christian and Muslim, thought it was a crucifix, a Christian image of a figure on a cross. Evans linked it to images of a Greek goddess and enthusiastically labeled it the "Aphrodite of Knossos!" Mackenzie described it more factually as an "earthenware hand-polished and incised figurine of a female without legs but with the broken surface, where they joined the body, traceable." Throughout their years at Knossos, Evans would make bold leaps of imagination, while Mackenzie would focus on the facts at hand.

Within a few days the diggers exposed the walls and floor of a building. By the end of the first week they found the remains of several rooms and corridors. They also found a tablet of baked clay, marked with unfamiliar symbols—the first example of writing from Knossos. Soon they would find a deposit of about 700 such tablets bearing two different varieties of symbols arranged in rows, or lines. Evans called these two unknown scripts Linear A and Linear B.

"A great day!" begins Evans's diary entry for April 5, 1900. On that day the excavators found pieces of a fresco bearing a human image. Evans interpreted this figure as a woman. He began calling her "Ariadne" after the legendary daughter of King Minos. The more cautious Mackenzie simply described the head, arms, and clothing of the figure, and concluded it could have been either a woman or a young man.

By this time Evans was already referring to the rooms that had been excavated as a set of royal apartments. In a telegram to the *London Times*, he reported that the ruin he was uncovering was "certainly a palace." Evans became more certain of this when the workers finished clearing a chamber that he had been calling a "bath chamber" because it contained a sunken tank similar to a tub. Further excavation revealed the remains of walls decorated

Evans desperately wanted to read the clay tablets— such as this one, inscribed in the script that he called Linear B script. The solution to Linear B, however, came after Evans's death. Another written language from Knossos, Linear A, remains a mystery.

with frescoes of plants. Against one wall was a single stone seat with graceful, curved legs and a high, carved back. Evans leaped to the conclusion that this "seat of honour or throne" had been made for a woman's full skirts and that the chamber must have belonged to the queen. He called it "Ariadne's bath."

Before long, however, Evans decided that the chamber must have been the king's throne room. When other archaeologists visited the site, he proudly showed them "the oldest throne in Europe." Evans declared that the tank was a lustral basin, which was filled with water for kings or priests to use for ritual purifications. Soon Evans was referring to the ruin as "the palace of King Minos."

Evans surveys the Throne Room. At first he thought it was a queen's bathchamber, but he came to believe that it may have been the throne room of the legendary King Minos himself.

At the end of May, Evans closed the site and returned to his estate in England, setting a pattern he repeated for many years. Work at the site began in February or March, when the winter rains ended, and continued through May or into June, until heat and the risks of malaria brought work to a close. The archaeologists spent the rest of the year examining their finds and writing reports. During the digging season they lived in a nearby *taverna*, or inn, until 1906, when Evans built the Villa Ariadne, a house overlooking the site that served as excavation headquarters.

By the end of the first season the diggers had uncovered more than two acres (87,000 square feet) of ruins—chambers, hallways, and stone-paved courtyards—all interconnected. Eventually the vast main structure at Knossos would prove to cover more than six acres, with more than 1,400 rooms. Evans wisely sought the help of an architect who examined traces, such as toppled walls and the broken bases of columns, and projected from them how the complete structures once looked.

During the second excavation season in 1901, the team unearthed a small table whose surface was a game board, inlaid with pieces of crystal, gold, silver, ivory, faience, or glazed clay, and plaster. Thousands of years ago people sat around it to play a game that may have resembled chess or backgammon. Evans considered the table one of the most spectacular artifacts ever found at Knossos. The second season also revealed many frescoes, including one called *The Bull Leapers*. Bronze and ivory figurines of bulls and leapers also came to light.

The last major discovery of the second season was the Grand Staircase. On the east side of the central courtyard the diggers uncovered broad steps that appeared to continue down into the ground. Believing that the staircase might be preserved on more than one level, Evans ordered it carefully excavated by experienced tunnel-workers. They dug down four flights of stairs, using boards to prop up the stairs above them as they went. The survival of the staircase was a stroke of luck. It had been built partly into the side of a hill, its framework of square wooden beams supported by earth and stones. The wood had decayed slowly, allowing time for dirt and rubble, such as fallen ceilings from the upper floors, to settle gradually against the stairway's walls, supporting them. Otherwise the walls would have collapsed.

As soon as the diggers began removing the packed rubble of past centuries, the staircase began to fall apart. Work halted at once. Then Evans's architect solved the problem by giving the staircase a new skeleton. He ordered wooden beams cut to the same sizes as

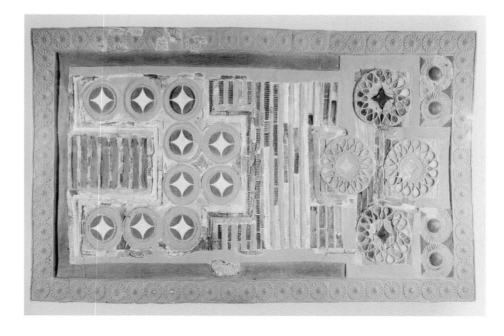

The rules of the game are unknown, but this spectacular find from Knossos is evidence that the Minoans played board games. The board, made in part of costly materials such as gold and ivory, is similar to game boards found in ancient Egyptian tombs.

those that had once held the staircase together. The cavities left by the decayed beams were painstakingly cleared out and the new beams carefully inserted before the bulk of the rubble was cleared. In this way the three-story stairway, one of the most spectacular features of the ruins, was preserved.

The 1902 season, during which Evans employed as many as 250 workers at a time, yielded pieces of some important frescoes. Diggers also unearthed small faience plaques, earthenware decorated with colored glazes—possibly ornaments—shaped like the fronts of two- and three-story houses. Architectural details such as windows,

The rebuilding of the Grand Staircase was one of the greatest technical challenges that Evans faced at Knossos.

Evans used small images of buildings as clues about the colors and architectural structures of the rooms and walls at Knossos. The dark horizontal lines may represent tie-beams that were inserted into these buildings for protection against earthquakes.

columns, and the ends of beams were clearly visible in these plaques.

Returning in 1903, the excavators made a significant find. Raising the stone floor slabs of a room just off the central courtyard, they found two cists, underground chambers used for burial or storage, containing many artifacts made of gold, stone, and faience. One object was part of a small statue of a woman whom Evans dubbed the Snake Goddess because of the serpents writhing around her arms and waist. She was not the only figure found at Knossos. Other figurines, as well as seals and frescoes, depict women whom Evans and later archaeologists have identified as goddesses or priestesses.

As the Knossos excavation progressed, Arthur Evans seethed with questions and ideas about the creators of all of these artifacts, pictures, and symbols—not to mention the sprawling palace itself. Before he began digging, Evans had believed that Crete had been part of the Mycenaean civilization unearthed by Schliemann on the Greek mainland. Before long, however, Evans realized that most of the artworks, objects, and architecture at Knossos were quite different from those of Mycenae. Although evidence suggested that Knossos had had some connections with both Mycenae and Egypt, its culture was neither Mycenaean nor Egyptian. The people who had lived in this palace were something new to history. Evans called them Minoans after King Minos.

3

In Search of the Minoans

By 1905 Evans was convinced that the Minoan civilization was older than the Mycenaean. He began weaving a picture of the Minoans' world and their history from what he found at Knossos.

Discoveries at other Cretan sites helped Evans shape his picture of the Minoans and their society. In 1903, the Italians found an ancient sarcophagus, or burial box, at another excavation in Crete. Dating from approximately 1400 B.C.E., it is painted with scenes of sacred rituals, such as the sacrifice of a bull and people offering calves and flowers at altars. An image of a tree sprouting from a shrine may represent rebirth and renewal. Powerful symbols, including horns, double-bladed axes, and tombs, adorn the sarcophagus. Evans believed that these images showed how the Minoans had looked and acted during their religious ceremonies; they also gave him ideas about the beliefs behind those ceremonies. He concluded that the central figure in Minoan religion was a mother-goddess, bringer of life and fertility to plants, animals, and humans. Her male companion, sometimes portrayed as a hunter, was a version of a mythological figure known as the Master of Animals, who is found throughout the ancient eastern Mediterranean.

While Evans pieced together his view of Minoan society, the excavations at Knossos continued. From the start, the archaeologists

This Cretan labrys, or double axe, dates from 1700 to 1600 B.C.E. At Knossos the image of double axe is scratched, carved, or painted onto many surfaces. Evans thought that the word "labyrinth" originally referred not to a maze but to this symbol. He argued that labyrinthos was a form of ancient Greek words meaning "House of the Double Axe" (labrys = "double axe"; inthos = "house").

Evans believed that images from sarcophaguses held clues to the Minoans' religious rites. This sarcophagus, or burial box, is covered with painted plaster. At the center is a scene of a bull sacrifice. The bull lies on the table already dead as two goats below the table wait a similar fate. At the right is the image of libation, or pouring of liquid offerings to the gods.

had to protect the site. Ruins that had survived for thousands of years covered by earth could deteriorate quickly when exposed to weather. The Minoans had built with mud-brick and limestone, sandstone, and gypsum, which are fairly soft and easy to cut. These materials crumble and erode faster than harder minerals. In 1901 Evans built a roof over the Throne Room to protect its gypsum seat and floor.

Some of the measures the excavation team had used to protect and restore the ruins became problematic. At the start of the 1905 season, they found that the timbers they had used to shore up the

Grand Staircase just a few years earlier had already rotted. They repaired the staircase immediately, this time using iron beams.

From the start of his excavations, Arthur Evans wanted to restore the palace, at least in part, to its bygone appearance. This task was made easier by the fact that parts of the structure, such as the Grand Staircase, had survived more or less intact. And the surviving pieces of frescoes not only showed how the palace had once been decorated but sometimes offered clues about its architecture as well. A fresco found in the northern part of the palace, for example, had a picture of a building, perhaps the palace itself. The structure's roofs were supported by smooth round columns that tapered slightly toward the bottom and were painted red and black. Evans rebuilt similar columns throughout the Knossos site. They are considered one of the most distinctive elements of Minoan architecture.

Thick columns, painted red and black and tapered toward the bottom, are characteristic features of the architecture of Knossos. Evans modeled these concrete pillars on columns shown in wall paintings at the site.

Bulls must have had important meaning in Minoan culture or belief. Their images appear on jewelry, wall paintings, and artifacts such as this rhyton, or drinking vessel. Like double axes, horned bulls appear to have been cult objects, associated with places of worship.

Archaeology at Knossos included restoration. Evans wanted people to be able to catch a glimpse of a long-dead culture. He treasured such experiences. Sleeping in the ruins one night, he imagined the familiar figures of the frescoes coming to life:

> [I was] tempted in the warm moonlight to look down the staircase-well, [and] the whole place seemed to awake awhile to life and movement. Such was the force of the illusion that the Priest-King with his plumed lily crown, great ladies, tightly girdled, flounced and corseted, long-stoled priests, and, after them, a retinue of elegant but sinewy youths—as if the Cupbearer and his fellows had stepped down from the walls—passed and repassed on the flights below.

Reconstruction was not easy. Evans had to draw upon evidence and imagination to envision how the palace's rooms had once looked. Parts of the palace were extensively reworked—Evans rebuilt and redecorated the Throne Room three times in all as he changed his ideas about how the Minoans had used the room.

Materials posed another challenge. At first Evans rebuilt with brick and wood, materials close to those the Minoans had used. He then used stronger and more permanent materials: steel beams and, during the 1920s, reinforced concrete. The final version of the Throne Room complex dates from this period. Evans also hired artists to paint new frescoes on many of the walls at Knossos based on surviving fragments of the ancient frescoes, which were carefully removed and preserved.

As Evans admitted in 1926, the scope of the reconstructions startled observers used to ruins that were . . . well, ruined. "To the casual visitor," Evans told the Society of Antiquaries, "the attempt may well at times seem overbold, and the lover of picturesque ruins may receive a shock." A French archaeologist named René

During the 1920s Evans finally completed his reconstruction of the Throne Room, which he had envisioned in a variety of ways. He was fascinated by the chamber's high-backed stone chair, calling it "the oldest throne in Europe"—although there is no real evidence that it was a royal seat.

Dussaud was one of many who criticized Evans's reconstruction, saying, "this clever archaeologist is completely rebuilding the palace of Minos from scratch." Some scholars feared that inaccurate reconstructions might obscure the site's true meaning.

Evans's restorations are controversial, but they have positive aspects. Knossos is impressive partly because, thanks to Evans, it is the one Minoan site that is more than a jumble of floors, steps, pits, and low, crumbled walls. Like the Pyramids of Egypt or the Colosseum of Rome, Knossos lets visitors see and feel what it was like to inhabit an ancient structure. Archaeologist Eleni Hatzaki, curator of the BSA at Knossos, points out that Evans's actions preserved Knossos. If he had simply excavated and described what he found, important features such as the Grand Staircase would have been lost.

Archaeological Stratigraphy

Evans and Mackenzie adopted a fairly new technique called archaeo-logical stratigraphy, which means identifying things by the strata, or layers of earth, in which they appear. Each stratum is older than the one above it and more recent than the one below it. Earth from the Knossos site was removed one stratum at a time—the features of each layer documented and the depth and position of every artifact recorded, down to slivers of broken pottery. This allowed Evans to compare the ages of different objects and identify various eras in the history of the site.

Like many ancient archaeological sites, Knossos was really several sites, one on top of another. Over the centuries, its inhabitants had built new structures on the rubble of old ones caused by some form of destruction. Evidence of charred wood was a sign of fire. Collapsed walls were signs of earthquake destruction, which Crete often experiences. Evans, who lived through an earthquake there, speculated that the roaring noise of such events may have seemed to the Minoans like "the bellowing of the bull beneath the earth," perhaps contributing to the Minotaur myth.

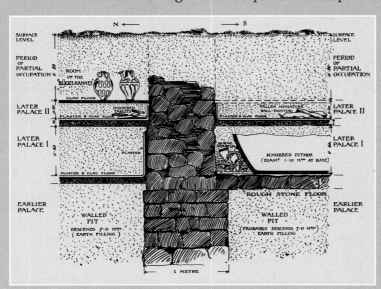

A 1903 article by Evans featured a stratigraphic drawing showing the ruins' many levels. Scientists now know that settlement at Knossos dates from about 7000 B.C.E. Kephala hill consists of layers of Stone Age settlements, the remains of thousands of years' worth of mud-brick dwellings, and the litter of human occupation.

4

Knossos Today

Evans's discoveries at Knossos stimulated archaeological interest in Crete and rewrote Aegean prehistory by revealing the existence of an unsuspected civilization. These finds also received much publicity in the popular press, and the world fell in love with the Minoans.

Each year, upon returning to England from Crete, Evans wrote scholarly and technical articles and delivered lectures to archaeological and historical societies. He also introduced the Minoans to the general public in articles for English newspapers, which American papers often reprinted.

Mount Juktas rises across the valley from Knossos. Archaeologists believe that people from the palace went to a sanctuary at the peak's summit for certain ceremonies. The focus of the sanctuary is a natural cave associated with Cretan Zeus, a deity somewhat different from the Zeus whom the later Greeks called the father of their gods. The Cretan Zeus was said to have died and been buried on Crete, perhaps in the cave on Mount Juktas.

People became fascinated with the surprisingly sophisticated quality of life at Knossos. Evans discovered evidence of architectural features unknown to the Greeks: shafts and transoms that brought sunlight and fresh air into the lower floors of the palace; adjustable doors that let residents control airflow; and a toilet—an open-topped stone seat over a drainage trench.

People also responded with enthusiasm to Minoan art. The wall paintings of Knossos were easy and natural in style. They showed people reveling in sports, leisure, and the natural world. Minoan art also reflected close observation and appreciation of nature, especially the sea. Pottery and sealstones offered such endearing details as an octopus shyly peering from a cleft among weed-covered rocks.

Evans's vision of Minoans was of cultured, pleasure-loving folk who dwelt peacefully in unfortified communities, protected by a

The plumbing of Knossos was extensive and elaborate. This stone drain is part of a system that carried rainfall and waste out of the palace complex.

navy and enriched by a trading fleet. Fellow British archaeologist Leonard Woolley saw in them "the most complete acceptance of the grace of life the world has ever known." Popular books such as James Baikie's 1907 *The Sea-Kings of Crete* and newspaper stories with headlines such as "The Fairy Tale of Ancient Crete" spread this image. They also reinforced Evans's identification of Knossos as "the palace of Minos." Although no evidence of a king named Minos or a labyrinth ever surfaced at Knossos, the world accepted the notion that Evans, like Schliemann at Troy, had found the actual historical source of an ancient myth.

Many Minoan artifacts are decorated with colorful images of marine life. Although Knossos was not a seaport, the Mediterranean was nearby, and the Minoans were clearly familiar with it and its inhabitants.

Since Evans's time, discoveries have led some historians to reconsider his view of the Minoans. Evans believed that the Minoans had had no military or defensive architecture, but Greek archaeologists have found the remains of Minoan-era stone forts across the Cretan countryside. This means that the Cretans likely engaged in warfare or at least in defensive activities. A discovery in 1979 suggests that they may also have conducted human sacrifices. British archaeologist Peter Warren and his Greek colleagues Jannis and Efi Sakellaris, working at Knossos and on the nearby peak of Mount Juktas, discovered ancient human bones, including those of several children, in circumstances that suggest they were sacrificed and possibly butchered. Could the Minoans have practiced ritual cannibalism? The suggestion provoked a storm of controversy, and only further research will answer the question.

Upon Evans's death the site passed into the control of the British School at Athens, which in the 1950s turned ownership

Layer upon layer, room crowded next to room, the palace of Knossos sprawled over more than six acres in its heyday. Today much of the site lies open to the air, but it is still a maze. Maps and plans help visitors navigate its corridors, staircases, and courtyards.

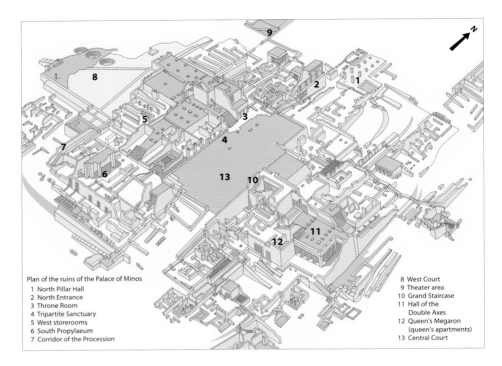

Plan of the ruins of the Palace of Minos
1 North Pillar Hall
2 North Entrance
3 Throne Room
4 Tripartite Sanctuary
5 West storerooms
6 South Propylaeum
7 Corridor of the Procession
8 West Court
9 Theater area
10 Grand Staircase
11 Hall of the Double Axes
12 Queen's Megaron (queen's apartments)
13 Central Court

over to the Greek government. Since then teams of archaeologists working at Knossos have excavated and studied the Stone Age settlement that preceded the town and palace, graves from the Mycenaean period, and Roman villas built centuries after the Minoan era.

Knossos is as fascinating today as when Arthur Evans excavated it. It is the second-most-visited archaeological site in Greece (after the Acropolis, the temple-crowned hill in Athens). A million people pass through its gates each year.

Knossos today is a mixture of ruins—mostly foundations and low, partial walls marking the dimensions of former rooms—and restored and repainted staircases, porticos, and chambers. The structure is organized around the central court, a stone-paved open space approached by a pillared entranceway on the north. Around the court spreads a mass of rooms and hallways, some dug into the hill, some stacked atop lower levels, linked with ramps and staircases. On the east side of the court, the Grand Staircase spans a multi-level complex believed to have been the royal residences.

Major features on the west side include the Throne Room, a hallway decorated with frescoes of Minoan figures, and storerooms. Beyond them, on the outer edge of the palace, is the West Court. Archaeologists think that this was a setting for ceremonies and also the official approach to the palace. Modern visitors enter the site from this direction. On the way they pass a bronze bust of Evans, gazing eternally at his remarkable discovery.

At its largest, Knossos may have housed hundreds or even thousands of people, including soldiers, religious functionaries, bureaucrats who tracked the flow of goods, and servants. It had storehouses for goods and workshops for the artists and craftspeople who produced such wares as pottery, jewelry, and bronze daggers. And as curator Hatzaki points out, many rooms had different uses in different eras. "The palace was actively used for nine hundred years," she says. "You can't speak of one palace, one function."

Every visitor marvels at the vivid and lovely frescoes of Knossos. They are the only such artworks found in Crete. The original frescoes that Evans excavated are now in the Archaeological Museum in Heraklion. Today experts are reexamining these originals and finding that some of Evans's interpretations were wrong. The dolphin fresco that he placed above a doorway in the queen's apartments is now thought to have been part of a collapsed plaster floor. Evans formed an image of a blue-painted man picking vegetation from six fragments and called it *The Saffron Gatherer*. Scientists found that

Vivid and energetic, this wall painting of leaping dolphins became a symbol of the popular view of the Minoans as artistic, playful nature-lovers. Just as modern archaeologists have revised that view somewhat, they have also questioned the accuracy of Evans's reconstruction of the painting. He filled in many gaps, leading some experts to suggest that the image is more Evans than Minoan.

the fragments really depict a blue monkey gamboling across a field. One of the best-known Minoan frescoes shows an elegant striding figure with flowing black hair and an elaborate plumed headdress. Evans called him *The Prince of the Lilies*, but, says Hatzaki, "There is no prince of the lilies." The plume may belong to a fresco of a griffin, and the prince's torso may have been part of a female figure.

As Arthur Evans excavated Knossos, he consciously amassed materials, including excavation records and a huge collection of pottery pieces, for future study by other archaeologists. Scientists now find rich ground for research in these materials. Using computers and technology for testing materials, for example, researchers examine pottery for such details as the mineral content of the clay. Knowing where in the ancient world items originated helps illuminate trade routes.

Evans reconstructed fragments of frescoes into an image of a man picking vegetation and called it The Saffron Gatherer (top) but archaeologists now believe that it originally depicted a monkey (bottom), not a man gathering flowers. The science of archaeology calls for the careful examination not just of ancient ruins but also of the ideas and interpretations of previous generations of scholars.

Archaeologists have learned much about the Minoans and Aegean prehistory since Evans's time, but much remains to be learned. If Linear A is ever deciphered, it may help scholars understand Minoans better. Linear A is thought to be the written form of the Minoan language. Experts do not know what this language was, but some Minoan words were incorporated into the Linear B tablets, which are written in Mycenaean, an early form of Greek.

The task of preservation Evans began continues today. Ironically, those in charge of protecting Knossos must now work to preserve both the ancient palace *and* Evans's reconstructions. By rebuilding with iron, steel, and concrete on top of old materials, such as soft stone and mud brick, Evans caused the ancient foundations and walls to withstand pressure that they were not designed to bear. To make matters more difficult, the iron Evans used is now rusting and the concrete is crumbling. Conservators must repair and replace his creations while protecting the underlying Minoan materials from weathering further.

Until the 1990s tourists clambered across Knossos without restriction, jumping on walls and rubbing exposed surfaces. Some people even picked up or chipped off bits of stonework as souvenirs. Today barriers keep visitors from the most worn parts of the site, such as the Grand Staircase and the royal apartments, although these can be viewed from other vantage points.

On June 8, 1900, near the end of his first season of excavation at Knossos, Arthur Evans sent a message to the offices of the *Athenaeum*, a scholarly journal in London. He had already announced that he had found ruins from the Mycenaean period at Knossos, but now he declared positively that he had located "the palace of Minos." Whether or not Minos really existed and ruled at Knossos, the ruins on Kephala hill today are known by the name Evans gave them. Evans opened a window into the Minoan past, and scholars, students, and tourists will always be eager to peer through that window.

Cracking the Code

After World War II ended in 1945, architect Michael Ventris spent his spare time studying Linear B, an undeciphered language from Knossos. He approached Linear B as syllabic writing, in which symbols called syllabograms represent combinations of consonants with vowels. The syllabograms are combined to form words. He also identified ideograms, or symbols representing recognizable things, such as horses or wine jars. Still, Ventris did not have enough information.

Then he speculated that the language of the text might be Greek. He thought the word next to an ideogram of a horse might mean "horse," and he identified its syllabograms with the syllables in the Greek word for horse. He could then read these syllabograms in other words and he began recognizing Greek words in the Linear B texts. No one had suspected that written Greek had existed so long ago. But Ventris and a classicist named John Chadwick finished deciphering Linear B, proving that it is an ancient form of Greek (sometimes called Mycenaean).

The grid shows Michael Ventris's first attempt (blue letters) to link Linear B symbols (brown symbols) with Greek syllabograms (black letters), or consonant-and-noun combinations. He identified the symbols for Linear B tablet as writing in Mycenaean, an early form of Greek.

	A / A₂	AI / E	I	O	U
	JA	JE		JO	
F	WA	WE	WI	WO	
G / K / CH	KA	KE / KE₂	KI	KO / KO₂	KU
T / TH	TA	TE / PTE	TI	TO	TU
D	DA / DA₂	DE	DI	DO	
P / PH / B	PA	PE	PI	PO	
KW / GW / CHW		QE		QO	
L / R	RA / RA₂	RE	RI	RO / RO₂	RU
M	MA	ME	MI	MO	
N	NA	NE	NI	NO	NU
S	SA	SE	SI	SO	

Interview with Chris Scarre

Rebecca Stefoff Did Minoan civilization arise on its own?

Chris Scarre For an island such as Crete, connections by sea with adjacent lands have always been important. The first settlers must have used boats to reach Crete, from Asia Minor, around 7000 B.C.E. Maritime connections continued in later periods and may have brought Cretans into contact with the early state societies of Egypt and the Near East. There is clear evidence of this contact in the form of Egyptian objects on Crete, Syrian elephant ivory in the Minoan palace of Zakro, and Minoan-style frescoes in Egypt and the southern Levant. The Minoans seem also to have borrowed the Egyptian color scheme of red-brown for men, and pale skins for women, in their frescoes. But contact does not equal cause, and the Minoan civilization was above all a homegrown product. They may have taken ideas from overseas—such as, perhaps, the idea of writing—but Minoan scripts owe little or nothing to other scripts in use in the East Mediterranean. The origins of Minoan civilization undoubtedly lie in social and economic changes on the island of Crete itself.

RS Evans and other writers of his day—and the general public, in fact—seem to have viewed the Minoans as something very

Archaeologist Chris Scarre (top) and writer Rebecca Stefoff (bottom, at Knossos).

different from other ancient peoples, with a highly distinctive culture and world-view. Were they really that different? What are the distinguishing features of Minoan civilization as apart from, say, Egyptian or Mycenaean?

CS Some of Evans's views about the nature of Minoan society now seem to us to be wishful thinking on his part. He thought, for instance, that the Minoans were a peace-loving people, in contrast to the militaristic Mycenaeans. But recent years have seen a growing awareness of Minoan weaponry and defensive works. Another idea is that women held an unusually important place in Minoan society, and that the leading Minoan deity may have been a mother-goddess. This is inspired by the prominence of women in Minoan frescoes and figurines, but may also be misleading.

Any comparison between Minoan society and other early civilizations, such as Egypt or Mesopotamia, inevitably highlights both similarities and differences. Ancient Egypt is famous for its elaborate funerary architecture; Minoan Crete is not without burials, but has nothing to rival the pyramids. Equally, the Minoan palaces are unlike anything we know from Egypt; indeed, the evidence of ritual activities at Knossos and other sites suggests they were much more than royal residences, and the word "palace" may be hindering us from appreciating their true nature.

RS Evans called the chair at Knossos "the oldest throne in Europe." Does it make sense to think of the Minoans as Europeans?

CS I think one thing that has clouded the interpretation of Minoan Crete is the idea that it constitutes the first European civilization, a term which suggests that it should somehow seem more familiar to us than the "non-European" civilizations of Egypt, the Near East, or, say, ancient China or Mesoamerica. But Minoan Crete had much closer links with North Africa and Asia Minor than it did with the bulk of Europe, and the idea that there is some kind of "European identity" that can be traced thousands of years back into the past is highly subjective. Minoan Crete should be seen as just one of several East Mediterranean Bronze Age state societies, distinct from the others in many ways, but also sharing many features with its neighbors.

RS What question would you most like to have answered, or archaeological mystery solved, about the Minoans or Knossos?

CS Wouldn't it be wonderful if we could be transported back in time to Knossos when the palace was a going concern? Anyone who has visited Knossos, or read about the site, must be intrigued by the theories and uncertainties over what really went on there. Did the Minoans really gather to watch bull-leaping performances in the palace courtyard? Was the palace the residence of a ruling dynasty, as Evans proposed, or was it more like a cult center or monastery, as others have suggested? Many such questions may never be answered, but there is always the hope that one day we may learn how to read the Linear A script and discover Minoan documents that tell us about their history and society. Minoan archaeology would then undergo a revolution like that of Maya studies following the recent decipherment of Maya script. We might be able to reconstruct Minoan history, and discover who it was that lived at Knossos, and what role the palace played in the life of the island. And we might come to understand why the Classical Greeks believed in a legend of the labyrinth and the Minotaur.

The Corridor of the Procession displays the Procession fresco, which depicts individuals carrying objects to a religious rite. In the fresco a Cupbearer on the right holds a conical rhyton, a ritual vessel used for libation.

Glossary

antiquities Physical relics of earlier ages.

artifacts Items made by humans, such as tools, coins, furnishings, weapons, art objects, and utensils.

cist Small belowground chamber used for burial or storage.

classicist Scholar of the classical languages, Greek and Roman.

cult Ritualized worship of a particular god or goddess.

decipher To figure out the meaning of an unknown script.

excavator One who excavates (digs up or unearths).

faience Earthenware, such as pottery or clay beads, that is decorated with colored glazes (hard, glassy finishes).

fresco Artwork painted on plaster, such as on a wall.

lustral Used in ceremonial purification.

malaria Disease carried by mosquitoes, most common in hot climates with pools or swamps.

portico Hall or porch with columns, usually at an entrance.

prehistoric Having to do with prehistory, the time before written records.

sarcophagus Stone coffin or large stone box that encloses a coffin.

seismic Having to do with movements of earth, such as in earthquakes.

terrace Level surface built up onto or cut into a hillside, usually supported by a reinforced wall.

terracotta Baked clay.

villa Large house, usually in the country or on a big estate.

Further Reading

Brown, Ann. *Arthur Evans and the Palace of Minos.* Oxford: Ashmolean Museum, 1989.

Caselli, Giovanni. *In Search of Knossos: The Quest for the Minotaur's Labyrinth.* New York: Peter Bedrick, 1999.

Castleden, Rodney. *The Knossos Labyrinth: A New View of the "Palace of Minos" at Knossos.* London: Routledge, 1990.

————. *Minoans: Life in Bronze Age Crete.* London: Routledge, 1993.

Cotterell, Arthur. *The Minoan World.* New York: Scribners, 1980.

Cottrell, Leonard. *The Bull of Minos: The Discoveries of Schliemann and Evans.* New York: Facts On File, 1984.

Farnoux, Alexandre. *Knossos: Searching for the Legendary Palace of King Minos.* New York: Abrams, 1996.

Friedrich, Walter L. *Fire in the Sea: The Santorini Volcano.* Cambridge: Cambridge University Press, 2000.

Harrington, Spencer P. M. "Saving Knossos," *Archaeology,* January/February 1999.

Higgins, Reynold. *The Archaeology of Minoan Crete.* New York: Walck, 1973.

Hood, Sinclair. *The Minoans: The Story of Bronze Age Crete.* New York: Praeger, 1971.

Horwitz, Sylvia L. *The Find of a Lifetime: Sir Arthur Evans and the Discovery of Knossos.* New York: Viking, 1981.

MacGillivray, Joseph Alexander. *Minotaur: Sir Arthur Evans and the Archaeology of the Minoan Myth.* New York: Hill and Wang, 2000.

Sakellarakis, Jannis, and Efi Sapouna-Sakellarakis. "Drama of Death in a Minoan Temple," *National Geographic,* February 1981.

Time-Life Books. *Wondrous Realms of the Aegean.* Alexandria, Va.: Time-Life Books, 1993.

Warren, Peter. *The Aegean Civilizations.* New York: Peter Bedrick, 1989.

————. "Knossos: New Excavations and Discoveries," *Archaeology,* July/August 1984.

Related Sites

Around the time Evans and Mackenzie broke ground on the Kephala hill, Crete began to swarm with busy researchers and their hordes of diggers. Evans's delvings into the Minoan past were part of a shared burst of discovery, not an isolated venture. An Italian team began work in 1900 on the south coast of Crete, uncovering a palace at Phaistos and a villa at Aghia Triadha. Cretan archaeologists examined ancient villas and tombs in several locations. David Hogarth of the British School of Athens and other British archaeologists also worked at several sites, including mountain caves and the fringes of Knossos. American archaeologist Harriet Boyd led the excavation of Gournia, a Minoan town east of Knossos. These archaeologists knew one another, visited each other's digs, and frequently shared information.

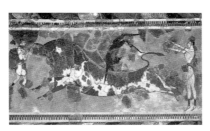

PHAISTOS

South coast of Crete, overlooking Mesara Bay

Two superimposed palaces on a low hill, they were arranged around a central court with a grand entrance, like Knossos, but lacked fresco decoration. The Late Minoan Phaistos palace was abandoned around 1480 B.C.E. The most famous find made at the site is the Phaistos Disk, a clay disk stamped with the spiraling signs of an early Cretan script not known from any other source.

MALLIA

North coast of Crete, 20 miles east of Heraklion

Third in importance of the Cretan palaces, Mallia has the Central Court, public rooms, and storerooms of the other palaces and is surrounded by buildings that show that the palace once stood at the heart of a small town. To the east was the cemetery, where a famous gold artifact in the shape of a wasp may have been discovered, and to the north was a harbor.

GOURNIA

North coast of Crete, on Mirabello Bay south of Agios Nikolaios

The most completely excavated Minoan town, a complex of narrow streets and houses are on a low hilltop. Formerly Gournia extended much farther up the modern shoreline. At the center of the excavated area is a paved square fronted on one side by the remains of an official building that may have been the residence of the local governor. The houses originally had upper floors, probably of timber-framed mud-brick.

PALAIKASTRO

East coast of Crete, 10 miles east of Siteia

A partially excavated Minoan harbor town, the second largest site known after Knossos, overlooked by the important Minoan mountain sanctuary of Petsophas. The houses of Palaikastro, grander and more elegant than those

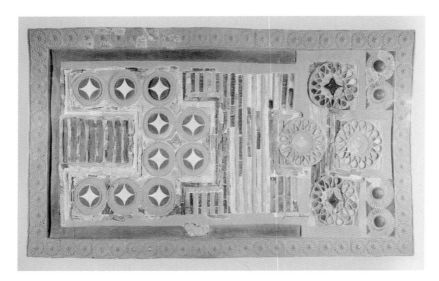

below the important hilltop shrine of Mount Juktas. One room held a wine press, and the presence of many storage jars suggests that this was the center of an agricultural estate. The high status of the building is shown by the use of carefully-selected building stone for paving and column bases.

MYRTOS-PYRGOS

South coast of Crete, 5 miles west of Ierapetra

A small Minoan hilltop settlement with extensive views over the Libyan Sea. Especially notable is the effective use of colored stone and the preserved gypsum paving of the grand house built at the center of the settlement during the Late Minoan period. At the western side of the hill, a paved road led down to an earlier two-story tomb.

of Gournia, are laid out in rectangular blocks separated by narrow streets. Some of the building stone came from a quarry not far to the east.

ZAKRO

East coast of Crete, 6 miles south of Palaikastro

Many-roomed houses of a small Minoan town crowd up against a Late Minoan palace with a central court, public rooms, and storerooms. The discovery in the site of elephant tusks from Syria shows that Zakro had important trade connections. There were also luxury objects, including carved stone *rhyta* (drinking vessels). The palace may have been added to (and partially built over) a pre-existing town.

VATHYPETRO

Central Crete, 5 miles south of Knossos

A "villa," or small palace, in the highlands of central Crete,

Index

Pictures and captions are indicated by page numbers in **bold**.

Archaeological Museum, Heraklion, 35
Ashmolean Museum, 10

Baikie, James, 33
Boyd, Harriet, 45
British School at Athens (BSA), 16, 29, 34, 45
Bull, bull-leaping, **8**–9, 20, **28**, 30, 42
Burials, **11**, 25, 34, 41

Central Court, 34–35, 45–46
Chadwick, John, 6, 39
Coins, 13–**14**
Cretan Exploration Fund, 16–**17**
Crete, 6–7, 9, 11–13, 15, 24–25, 30–31, 40–41, 45–46
Cupbearers, 28, **42**

Dolphin fresco, 35–**36**
Double axe. *See* Labrys.
Dussaud, René, 28–29

Evans, John Arthur, 6, **10**, **14**–31, 33, 35–36, 38, 41, 45
Evans, Margaret Freeman, 10, 15

Faience plaques, 23–**24**
Figurines, 18–20, 23–**24**, 41
Frescoes, 7, 18–20, 24, 27–28, 32, 35–**36**, 40–**42**

Game board, 20, **22**
Goddesses, **24**–25, 41
Grand Staircase, 21–**23**, 26–27, 29, 35, 38
Great Court, 8

Hatzaki, Eleni, 29, 35–36
Heraklion, 13–14, 35
Hogarth, David, 16, 45

Jars. *See* Pithoi.

Kalokairinos, Minos, 6, 13, 16, 18
Knossos, 6–**9**, 13, 15–**17**, 20, 25, 29–**31**, 34–35, 38, 41–42, 45

Labrys, **24**–**25**, **28**
Labyrinth, 12, **14**, 42
Linear A, Linear B script, 6, 18, 37–**39**, 42

Mackenzie, Duncan, 16, 18–19, 30, 45
Maze. *See* Labyrinth.
Minoans, Minoan civilization, 6–7, 9, **14**, 18, **22**, 24–**27**, **30**, 32–34, 37–41

Minos, 12, 24, 33, 38
Minotaur, 12, **14**, 30, 42
Mosaics, **12**
Mount Juktas, 33–**34**, 46
Mycenae, Mycenaeans, 7, 10–**11**, 14, 24, **38**, 41

Palace at Knossos, **9**–10, 13–14, **17**, 20, 27–29, **31**–33, 35, 38, 41–42
Palace of Minos at Knossos, The, 6
Palaces, Cretan, 7, 45–46
Phaistos Disk, 45
Pillars, **27**
Pithoi, **14**, 16, 18
Plumbing, **32**
Pottery, 15, 30, 32–**33**, 36
Preservation, 6, 22, 26–27, 29, 38
Priestess figurines, **24**
Prince of the Lilies, The, 36

Queen's apartments, 19, **21**, 35

Reconstructions, restorations, 6, 26–**29**, 34, **36**, 38
Rhyton, **28**
Royal apartments, residences, 19, 35, 38, 41

Saffron Gatherer, The, 35–**37**
Sakellaris, Efi and Jannis, 33

Sarcophagus, 25–**26**
Scarre, Chris, **40**–42
Schliemann, Heinrich, 6, 10–**11**, 13–14, 24, 33
Seals, sealstones, 14, 24
Snake Goddess, 23–**24**
Society of Antiquaries, 28
Stefoff, Rebecca, **40**–42
Storage jars. *See* Pithoi.
Storerooms, 18, 35, 45
Stratigraphy, **30**

Tablets, baked clay, 18, **38**
Theseus, 12
Throne Room, 7, **17**, 19–**20**, 26, 28–**29**, 35, 41
Timeline, 7
Trade routes, 36, 40
Troy, city of, 10, 13, 33

Villa Ariadne, 21
Ventris, Michael, 6, **39**

Wall paintings. *See* Frescoes.
Warren, Peter, 33
West Court, 35
Women, 14, **24**, 41
Woolley, Leonard, 33
Workshops, 35

Zeus, 11–12, **34**

Chris Scarre is a specialist in the prehistory of Europe and the Mediterranean, with a related interest in the ancient Near East and the classical world of Greece and Rome. He earned his MA and PhD at Cambridge, the latter based on a study of landscape change and archaeological sites in western France. He has excavated in France and Greece and has written a number of academic papers about megalithic tombs and French prehistory. He is currently Deputy Director of the McDonald Institute for Archaeological Research, University of Cambridge, and editor of the biannual *Cambridge Archaeological Journal*.

Rebecca Stefoff is the author of many books for young readers. History and science are among her favorite subjects. She has previously written about archaeology and the Minoans in *Finding the Lost Cities*.

Brian Fagan is Professor of Anthropology at the University of California, Santa Barbara. He is internationally known for his books on archaeology, among them *The Adventure of Archaeology*, *The Rape of the Nile*, and *The Oxford Companion to Archaeology*.

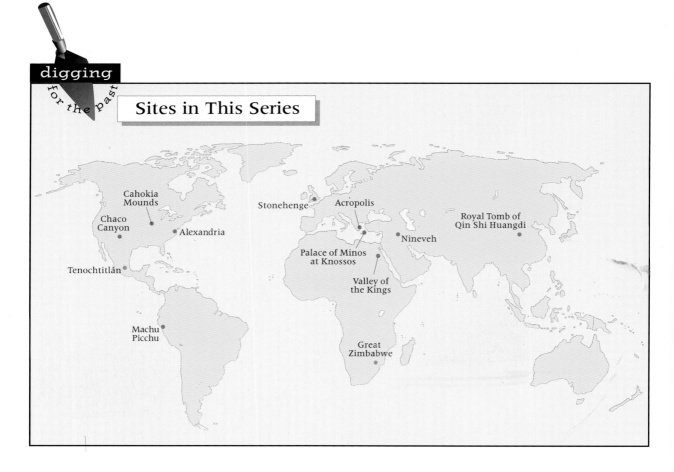

digging
for the past

Sites in This Series

Cahokia Mounds

Chaco Canyon

Alexandria

Tenochtitlán

Machu Picchu

Stonehenge

Acropolis

Palace of Minos at Knossos

Valley of the Kings

Nineveh

Royal Tomb of Qin Shi Huangdi

Great Zimbabwe